THIS BOOK BELONGS TO:

_____

DEDICATION

To my son Bodhi,
his classmates and amazing teachers.

Your love for these practices
has inspired these books.
You may be small
but you are mighty!

DINOSAURS HAVE
BIG FEELINGS
TOO

A mindful adventure
to help manage emotions
and get the inner roar out.

Enjoy adding sound effects
like roaring or stomping
while seated or standing.

THE ADVENTURE

One day in the jungle, on a cold wet damp day, Rex the T-Rex came stomping, stomp stomping, this way......

With his sharp teeth, big feet and small hands,
Rex was known as the king, the king of this land.

And as he looked at the trees
way up and way down,

the distracted T-Rex dropped
his gold crown.

"Oh no!"

He roared.
At first he was mad.
He roared so loud!

Rex needed help to pick up his crown off the ground.

So he looked around for a friend and then heard a strange sound...

THUMP

THUMP

THUMP

THUMP

It was Brock the Sauraus,
his HUGE 4-legged friend,

who fearlessly strutted with his
long neck he could easily bend.

AND...

Tara the Dactyl
who was high in the sky,
flew down very worried
at that strange-sounding cry.

AND...

Veloci the Raptor came running so fast.
He was so nervous and anxious he
nearly ran right past.

AND...

A scared little boy
from the village nearby,

bravely skipped over
to see what was that cry.

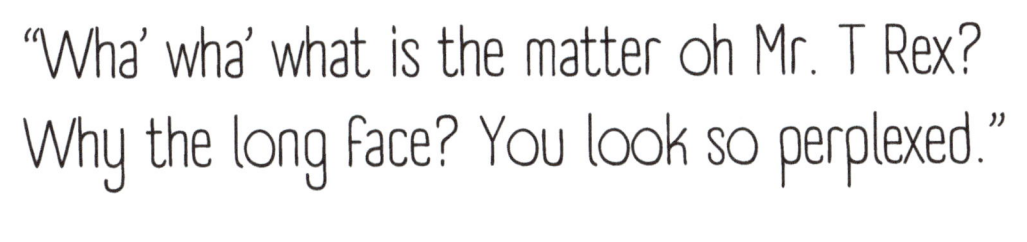

You see...
all of his friends normally
considered the king rude,
because all he normally considered
them to be was food.

But It was clear that Rex needed
help with something.
And each of his friends had a special
skill they could bring.

Tara's good sight from her height spotted the crown with ease.

And Brock's long bendy neck helped them all to see.

Veloci was so quick to find the spot where it dropped.

And the boy close to the ground
picked it right up.

After they all helped Rex so he wasn't so sad,
he smiled and apologized for getting so mad.

LET'S DO
THE FINGER HOLDS

Now join me. It doesn't matter how many fingers or claws you have: one, two, or three. You can sit or lie down comfortably.

First wrap your thumb like your hand is giving it a big hug. Don't squeeze too hard or even tug.

Take a deep breath in and big breath out.
And let any sadness get all the way out.

Now hug your index finger and don't feel afraid.
Breathe in and out again and feel extra brave....

Next, move to the middle finger and let go of any anger.
It's like roaring inside without any of the danger.

Let's slow down and hold the ring finger next.
Breathe in and out again to feel calm and relaxed.

Now last but not least hold the pinkie finger too.
Give yourself a smile at all the amazing things
you can do.

"Thank you for helping us feel better!"

All the dinosaurs roared.

Rex was so grateful his mood had improved.
Now he knows what to do to be a cool king dude.

Brock the Sauraus held his head high in the sky.
And bravely strutted away as Tara said bye.

Veloci slowly walked away happy to not be in a hurry.
And the brave boy waved goodbye no longer worried.

Rex smiled big and took a few deep breaths…

He was grateful for his friends and the meal he happily skipped.

DISCUSS AND LEARN MORE

Even animals have feelings. Do you remember what the dinosaurs were feeling?

Rex was angry and sad

Tara and Veloci were worried and anxious

Brock was fearless and curious

The Boy was scared and brave

Just like our friends: Rex, Brock, Tara, Veloci and the Boy we are all different and we feel things differently too.

What is a moment when you had these feelings?

Did you get more like Rex? Did you roar?

Did you get angry or sad?

Or did you feel anxious, scared or lonely?

The Finger Holds to Manage Emotions can help you control your feelings instead of them controlling you!

And.....
(luckily we have more fingers than a T-Rex!!)

Children can hold as little as 30 seconds to 1 minute.
Adults might need to hold 2-5 minutes.

You can also hold another person's finger if they are unable to hold their own.

The Finger Hold Practice

Hold each finger, in turn, with the other hand, holding for as long as it feels comfortable or until you feel a pulse. Either hand is acceptable and you can also work with just one or two fingers if that feels most helpful.

While holding gently, but firmly, breathe naturally. Release any tension or stored emotions on the exhale, then move to the next finger until you have done all of them.

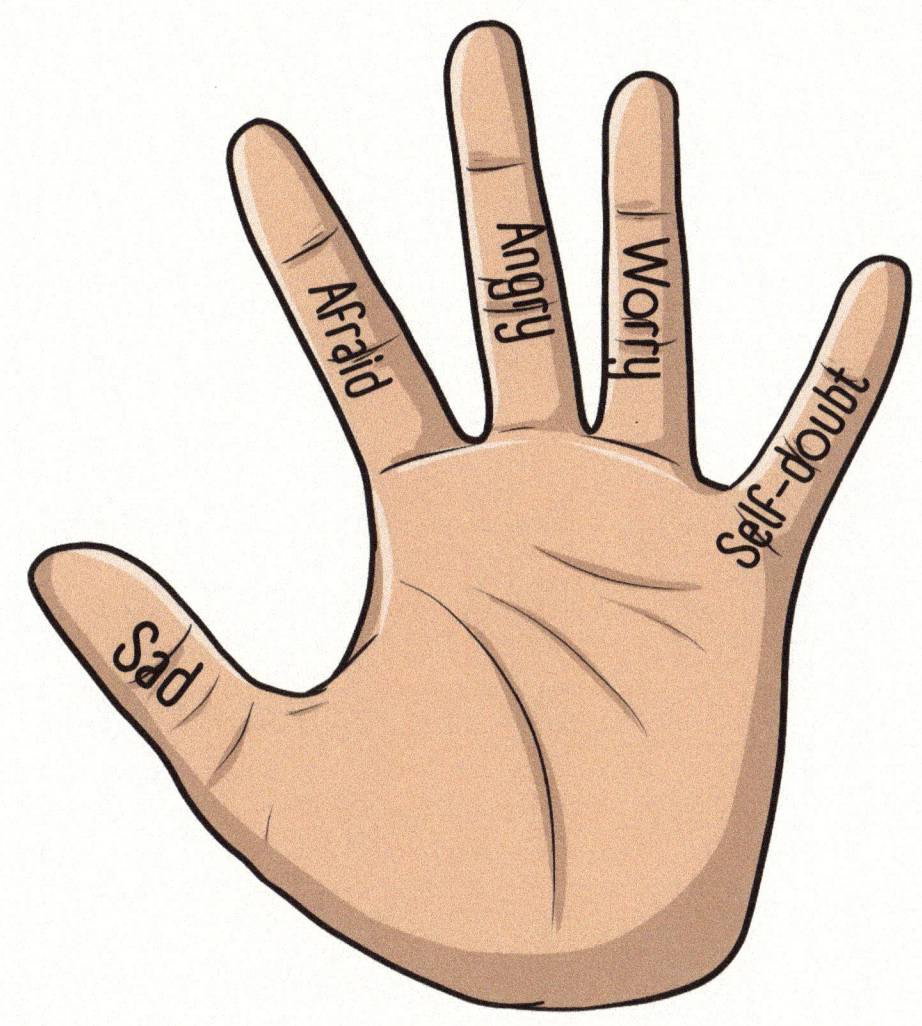

Key:
Thumb — tears, sadness, upset
Pointer/Index finger — fear, panic, scared
Middle finger — anger, rage, impatience
Ring finger — worry, stress, anxiety
Little finger — self-doubt, low self-esteem

Affirmations:
Thumb — I am okay
Pointer/Index finger — I am brave
Middle finger — I am chilled out
Ring finger — I am calm and relaxed
Little finger — I believe in myself

ABOUT THE AUTHOR

Taran Collis AWC, C-IAYT has been teaching therapeutic yoga and wellness education for over 20 years. Taran's passion is educating adults and children through multicultural practices that inspire a love for self-care. She enjoys creating mindfulness stories and guided imagery that spark joy and imagination in young and older readers alike.

Capacitar International - The Finger Holds To Manage Emotions are available in 41 different languages at www.capacitarinternational.org